INSTRUCTIONS:

1 BREATHE
Take a deep breath

2 BREATHE AGAIN
Now take another

3 PENS, PENCILS, CRAYONS
Get your coloring supplies; pens, pencils, or crayons

4 ZONE OUT
Forget the outside world

5 ANYTHING GOES
Start and stop wherever you want in the book

 THIS IS YOUR TIME *enjoy!*

true love

&

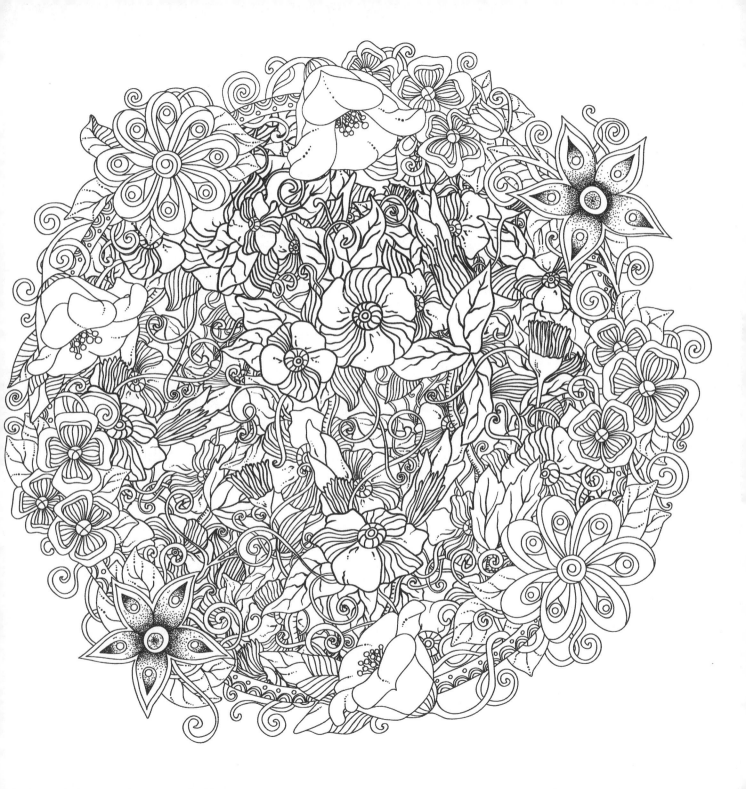

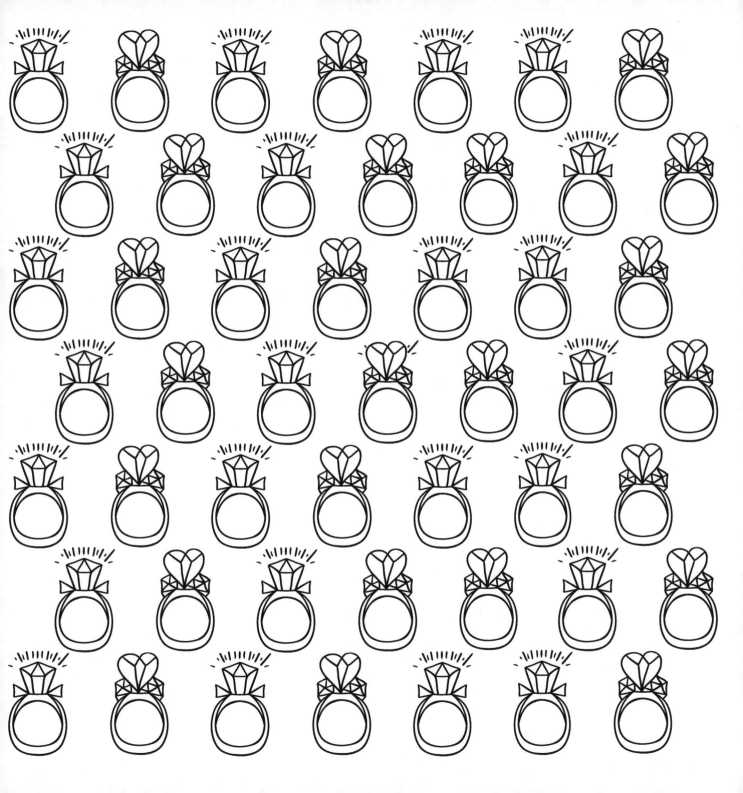

Made in the USA
San Bernardino, CA
14 March 2016